Jump Start

The Believer's Beginning Guide to Financial Freedom

Darneisha Petit-Beau

Copyright © 2021 by Darneisha Petit-Beau

All Scripture quotations, unless otherwise indicated, are taken from the King James Version of the Holy Bible.

All rights reserved. No part of this publication may be reproduced, stored in a retrieval system, or transmitted in any form or by any means, electronic, mechanical, photocopy, recording, or any other, except for brief quotation in printed reviews, without prior permission of the author.

CONTENTS

Foreword 1

Your Financial Roadmap 4

Managing Your Resources Wisely 17

Building Generational Wealth 26

Afterthought 67

Foreword

First, I want to congratulate you as you embark on your journey to financial freedom! This freedom extends beyond money, but it is an opportunity to be available as a resource to benefit the Kingdom! The Bible tells us that, "A good man leaves an inheritance to his children's children." (Proverbs 13:22 NKJV) This begins with developing our mindset to manage and maintain the resources God has given us. I believe the foundation of legacy building rest on these three principles:

- Mindset
- Management
- Maintenance

Your mindset is the framework of how you think and ultimately, the reason for your decision making. Management and maintenance are essential because we are called to manage (handle with skill, be in charge of) and maintain (preserve) the things, and people if you have children, employees, etc given to us.

My purpose in writing this booklet is to help encourage you to overcome the financial pitfalls that many people face unnecessarily. We will briefly discuss each pillar of legacy building so that you may evaluate where you are and work to develop a plan to move forward.

As believers we tend to focus on the religious aspects of our walk, checking off the boxes off Christianity, never fully entering the place where God wants and needs us to be. Now is the time to shake off the old mindset! I only ask that you open your heart and your mind. Relax and take it easy, you are in good hands (Proverbs 1:33).

Do you have a desire to progress financially? Have you ever found yourself feeling down when the topic of finances surfaced?

Finances (and even talking about finances) can be a daunting task for many reasons; none of which is excusable to remain in ignorance. What you don't know can hurt you in many ways and my friends, ignorance is not bliss! Ignorance is a stumbling block and an explanation as to why many don't succeed. Many choose to remain ignorant because they don't know any other way. Our parents were ignorant, our friends are ignorant, and we are training our children to be ignorant as well. Now is the time to break the cycle!

First and foremost, we must seek after and cling to the knowledge of God. We must allow it to permeate our lives. It is not God's will for us to remain ignorant (Hosea 4:6). Seek Him first and all these things will be added to you (Matthew 6:33). While these things can be material, the addition of the desire and thirst for true intimacy with God should be high on our list of wants. To prosper, we must commit ourselves to the things of God. Are you familiar with King Solomon's story? King Solomon was a wise and successful businessman who sought the Lord daily for instruction (1 Kings 4:29-34). As you allow the wisdom of God to increase you in earthly wisdom, the Lord will teach you to succeed in every area of your life (Isaiah 48:17-18). Wisdom is your God-given birthright.

Your Financial Roadmap

Allan Laiken, a well-known author coined the phrase, "The failure to plan is planning for failure". To know where you are going, you must first know and understand where you are. Looking back on your life, whether it be the past six months, three years, or twelve years, do you think you would be in a better position financially if you had an effective plan in place? Many times, we live for the moment, spending, hoping, and praying for that million-dollar check to come in the mail, but have you ever considered that God's plan for you could be a little different? There were times when I would charge large unnecessary purchases in the months of December, January, or February because I knew I'd have my income tax refund coming. Was that wisdom? Not at all. Let's be clear, I am the first partaker of this. I have gone from having thousands in the bank to having nothing with thousands in debt and a prayer to keep my bills paid. It's taken time but I've worked my way back up & I'm FINALLY seeing the light. God is a miracle-working God. However, if His will is for you to grow into your prosperity, instead of that "and suddenly" blessing, then you must learn (as I have learned) to take the necessary steps. Let's take a look into them:

Step one:

Commit to living a life that is pleasing unto God. This statement in itself is a book on its own.

Step two:

Pray and ask God to lead you and guide you to make better choices financially. Create a plan. The key is to know where you are in order to plan and prepare for a successful future. Change bad habits and allow wisdom to lead you in your decision-making. If we are not wise stewards over our current finances how can we use wisdom in the overflow? Luke 16:10 (AMP) **begins** with, "He who is faithful in a very little [thing] is faithful also in much." Have you proven yourself trustworthy with your finances? If not it's ok! God is a merciful and forgiving God, make a commitment to make smarter choices today!

Consider the different ways that you can make smarter choices for the betterment of your finances. Let's start with giving. I am a firm believer in the principle of giving. Tithing is a very controversial subject among believers & non-believers because many refuse to believe that the sacrifice made by giving will reap a reward. I don't want to preach to the non-tithers, but you must understand that tithing requires faith to step in. Faith says "God, I trust YOU, not the pastor (or the church's board), with a tenth of my income because it is what is required of me". God has promised us that if we give Him just a dime out of the dollar we earn He will take care of us (Malachi 3:11). There may be times where we cannot have the things we want but God has promised that He will take care of what we need (Matthew 6:25-32).

Many non-believers participate in the principles established by God for His children and consistently reap the rewards of it. How much more can we, God's children, receive by giving a portion of what God has blessed us with back to Him without regret or complaints (2 Corinthians 9:7)? Remember, tithing is not meant to benefit God. He is more than capable of financing the mandates of His Kingdom without your money. The Earth is the Lord's and the fullness thereof (Psalm 24:1). Tithing is meant to benefit you! Your seed will speak for you. The Word of the Lord says to "Test me in this and see if I don't open up heaven itself to you and pour out blessings beyond your wildest dreams (Malachi 3:10). As I look back on my resume, I see that God has proven Himself faithful to me because I consistently pay my tithe and I sow as He leads me. This is a testament to God's faithfulness. Give and it shall be given unto you. All you have to do is trust Him!

Step three:

Evaluate your current financial situation. What do you do currently to observe your finances? Take some time to create a budget and set a few realistic goals. God is perfectly capable of performing miracles in your life. However, we must do our part and evaluate where we are to set realistic goals for where we what to go. We must progress as part of our learning process to avoid making the same mistakes we have made in the past.

List your current income (and your spouse's current income) and all of your current expenses (including your mortgage/rent to your child's extracurricular activities to the dry cleaning). Are you cringing because you see red? Are you in surplus? Do you see room for improvement? A common mistake, that I have also made, is to only list out the large expenses without taking into consideration those little expenses. The "innocent" amounts spent at Starbucks and the movies each month begins to add up. If you need a little help developing your budget, visit daveramsey.com and view the different, available budgeting resources. Use the "Quick Start" budget as a guideline to create your own personal budget. Once your budget is created, evaluate it. If you find that you have more than enough money left over then rejoice, pay off some debt, and save for the future. If you find that things are a little tight, or if you end up with more red than you'd like to see, look at where you can cut back on unnecessary spending. Does little Jamie have to attend the ballet, tap, and jazz class three times a month? Can you pack your lunch for work instead of eating out on your lunch break to save some extra funds? Small changes can make a very big difference!

Step four:

Reduce your debt. Are you holding on to faith that God will allow you to live a debt-free life? Start by paying off your debts. Make larger monthly payments that fit within your budget. If you are not quite at the point where you can make those payments, set a deadline for yourself, and commit to re-evaluating your budget. Make room for those payments, as they will frame your financial future. Some people attack one bill at a time without considering the fact that their other lingering debts are being reported to credit bureaus. Try eating the elephant piece by piece. Making small payments on every bill not only brings the balance down but also shows your creditor that you are trying to get caught up. With this method, fewer items are reported negatively on your credit, and you are also able to reduce the amount of interest paid on past due debts.

Obtain a copy of your credit score and verify the accuracy of the items listed. Contact any creditors to set up a payment plan that is within your budget and begin paying off debt. It may seem like you're facing a mountain, but remember that

God is bigger than that mountain! Start small. If you have school loans, there are payment options available to you at any income level. Contact your lender to discuss any forbearance, deferment, or income-based repayment options.

Step five:

Seek the advice of a trained professional (and read the rest of this book). A few years ago, I completed the Financial Peace University and it was life-changing. The Financial Peace University is an online or in-person course, created by Dave Ramsey, designed to teach you about the steps needed to succeed on your financial journey. As a Finance major it opened my eyes to view debt differently and gave me a new perspective on my finances. It helped reaffirm a few things that I was doing right, and it showed me where I was wrong. Take the class, it is a wise investment in your future.

Discipline is key if you plan on being successful on this financial journey to freedom. The hardest part is changing old habits and bad mindsets. I have learned that expecting and believing God to change your situation will require you to make some changes. I cannot have a slave mentality and expect to live like a King. I cannot be stingy with my finances and expect God to bless me exceedingly abundantly above what I could ask. The journey to prosperity will differ for each of us but the premise remains the same. Lean on and rely confidently upon God's ability to provide for you while you wisely choose to use the resources He has made available to you.

Changing Your Mindset

I am a firm believer that as Children of God we are entitled to the full benefits of His Kingdom! What good is it to be a prince or princess, but yet live with no access to your Kingdom? Many do not see results in their lives because they have not committed to serving God. This commitment extends beyond attending Sunday morning service and Wednesday night Bible study. The fruit that you bear is an indication of your relationship with God. What does your life say about you?

We cannot ignore the principles of the Word (including tithing) and willfully lack wisdom when it comes to our finances, and then expect a miracle manifestation. Miracles are for those who do not believe in God's precious promises. As believers, we should live our lives with the daily expectation of God's glory. We all experience different seasons and trials, but we are entitled to the Kingdom! You have to believe it in your heart. It is not a cliche or a tithe gimmick, it is a principle. The King has established and maintained your victory so that you can have, and enjoy, life in its abundance (John 10:10). "No one is perfect" is a true statement. However, it is not a reason to justify sin. A heart that is truly in a state of repentance does not excuse its sin. It works toward turning away from sin, which causes a separation between us and God. "No one can serve two masters; for either he will hate the one and love the other, or he will stand by and be devoted to the one and despise and be against the other. You cannot serve God and mammon, deceitful riches, money, and possessions (Matthew 6:24). We must renew our minds and step up to the task of mapping out a better financial future!

Renewing Your Mind

The Bible tells us to renew our minds daily because the mind is the most powerful tool that we have! You cannot control certain situations but you can control your mindset, your thoughts, and perspective toward that situation. You may hate your job but instead of waking up every morning complaining about your job, find the good in your situation. I went through a season where I dreaded going to my job. I was in tears some days because I felt like I could not handle the pressure from what was required in my position. One day, I decided to view my role as a challenge; a challenge to grow, develop skills, and strengthen my mental muscles in ways that had never been strengthened, or developed, before. Even today, I have had to force myself to choose to see the good in what I do. I have so many things to complain about but I refuse to focus on that or even engage in conversation that will deter my focus. I'm impacting lives and making a difference every day. This is the place where God has allowed me to be so He will strengthen me to compete and fulfill my assignment.

Our mindsets are framed by things that we have experienced in our past. They can also be framed by our childhood experiences, prior connections and relationships, and even our own mistakes. Scripture tells us to renew our mind because every single decision we make is a result of our mindset.

It is also important to be grateful in all things. Living life with a heart of gratitude is a reassurance to ourselves, and the rest of the world. When we are grateful God is granted the opportunity to further bless us through our humility.

There is something to be grateful for in every moment, regardless of your situation. Think about it! You may not be working your dream job yet, but at least you are not unemployed. You may not live in your dream home, but you are safe, protected, and with shelter. You could be facing a mountain of debt, but know that there is a way out!

Take a moment and write down three things that you are grateful for:

Saying "No"

There are many times where I have had to say "NO" to things that my heart ached for. That is self-control. In the book "As A Man Thinketh", James Allen states that, "A man should conceive of a legitimate purpose in his heart, and set out to accomplish it. He should make this purpose the centralizing point of his thoughts. It may take the form of a spiritual ideal, or it may be a worldly object, according to his nature at the time being; but whichever it is, he should steadily focus his thought forces upon the object which he has set before him. He should make this purpose his supreme duty and should devote himself to its attainment, not allowing his thoughts to wander away into ephemeral fancies, longings, and imaginings. This is the royal road to self-control and true concentration of thought. Even if he fails again and again to accomplish his purpose (as he necessarily must until weakness is overcome), the strength of character gained will be the measure of his true success, and this will form a new starting point for future power and triumph."

Oftentimes, friends and family will not understand the word "no", because they are very used to benefiting from your "yes". When you are creating a financial road map you may want to calculate the exact expenses that you have along with the finances needed to save and the residual. This way, you are not loaning out or spending more than you are receiving. If people ask for money that you cannot afford to spend out, tell them "I do not have money for that right now". If they ask you to go out to dinner and it's not in your budget, politely decline. Trust me, you will get push back, but your goals are bigger than the moment. Consider evaluating your relationships and friendships. Are they conducive to the life you want to live? Are they good influences on you on this journey to financial freedom? You may have to let some folks go and you must be ok with that. If they truly love you, they will understand.

Managing Your Resources Wisely

Dr. Myles Munroe once said, "Time is the most valuable commodity that you have". Time is so important because we do not know the time, nor the hour when our time (lives) will run out. I don't know about you, but I do not want to stand before the Lord having not had used my time wisely on Earth. Wouldn't that be scary? Think about what you have been giving your time to, what ponders your mind consistently? What do you spend most of your time doing? The answers to these questions will help you begin to become more conscious about how you spend your time. Author and creator of "High Performing Habits: How Extraordinary People Become That Way", Brendon Burchard, expressed that you can give your time to the drama and conflict of telling people they aren't what you want or need in life, or you can use that same time to build a new circle. One of the best ways to become more efficient with your time is to take stock of where you currently are, including your relationships, and set an action plan for moving forward.

Time Management

Have you ever wondered how some people seem to fit every single task into their day, remain rested, and still have time to do things at nighttime? That, my friend, is the practice of effective time management. Time management is defined as the ability to use one's time effectively or productively, especially at work. Time management is an essential part of wisdom. Failing to manage your time will cost you peace of mind, finances, opportunities, and sometimes even relationships. Proper time management allows you to work smarter rather than harder, enabling you to get much more done in much less time.

Proverbs 10:4 states, "A slack hand causes poverty, but the hand of the diligent makes rich." In other words, people who strive toward ensuring that every bit of their time is spent working toward their goals have more success than those who do not. Prioritizing is also very important. When you prioritize, you are easily able to see what can be put off and what urgently needs to be done this instant.

According to the Corporate Finance Institute, a few ways that you can manage your time effectively includes:

Set goals correctly

Set goals that are achievable and measurable. Use the SMART method when setting goals. In essence, make sure the goals you set are Specific, Measurable, Attainable, Relevant, and Timely.

Prioritize wisely

Prioritize tasks based on importance and urgency. For example, look at your daily tasks and determine which are:

Important and urgent: Do these tasks right away.

Important but not urgent: Decide when to do these tasks.

Urgent but not important: Delegate these tasks if possible.

Not urgent and not important: Set these aside to do later.

Set a time limit to complete a task

Setting time constraints for completing tasks helps you be more focused and efficient. Making the small extra effort to decide on how much time you need to allot for each task can also help you recognize potential problems before they arise. That way you can make plans for dealing with them.

For example, assume you need to write up five reviews in time for a meeting. However, you realize that you'll only be able to get four of them done in the time remaining before the meeting. If you become aware of this fact well in advance, you may be able to easily delegate writing up one of the reviews to someone else. However, if you hadn't bothered to do a time check on your tasks beforehand, you might have ended up not realizing your time problem until just an hour before the meeting. At that point, it might be considerably more difficult to find someone to delegate one of the reviews to, and more difficult for them to fit the task into their day, too.

Take a break between tasks

When doing a lot of tasks without a break, it is harder to stay focused and motivated. Allow some downtime between tasks to clear your head and refresh yourself. Consider grabbing a brief nap, going for a short walk, or meditating.

Organize yourself

Utilize your calendar for more long-term time management. Write down the deadlines for projects, or for tasks that are part of completing the overall project. Think about which days might be best to dedicate to specific tasks. For example, you might need to plan a meeting to discuss cash flow on a day when you know the company CFO is available.

Remove non-essential tasks/activities

It is important to remove excess activities or tasks. Determine what is significant and what deserves your time. Removing non-essential tasks/activities frees up more of your time to be spent on genuinely important things.

Plan ahead

Make sure you start every day with a clear idea of what you need to do – what needs to get done THAT DAY. Consider making it a habit to, at the end of each workday, go ahead and write out your "to-do" list for the next workday. That way you can hit the ground running the next morning.

Money Management

I like nice things. In the past, it would be very hard for me to turn away from the temptation of buying things that I did not need. I had to learn to delay the satisfaction of material things in order to ensure that priorities are taken care of. I like to call this "delayed gratification". Gratification is defined as the pleasurable emotional reaction of happiness in response to a fulfillment of a desire or goal. It is important that you don't allow the desire for material things to consume your finances so much that you deplete yourself of money that you actually need for bills and other important things. This is where your budget comes in. Review & refine your budget every few months or as often as needed to ensure that it fits in with your financial goals.

Personally, I like to budget this way:

60% toward bills

20% toward savings

10% toward tithes

10% toward personal spending

I created this budget based on where I am financially. The goal is to live **below** your means, living off less than what you actually make. I do this same thing with my family business. I want to mention that I do not always follow my budget in its entirety. As our business grew, we invested more into it and saved a little less. You must make small adjustments and changes as required. The bottom-line is, *every dollar spent without a specific assignment is a dollar wasted.* When we put a name to each of our dollars, we are able to tell our money what to do, instead of it being the other way around. Always make sure you pay your bills and your tithes first. Your tithes can be compared to a seed that is constantly being watered with a promise to grow fully and abundantly one day, by faith. Faith does not mean to overspend in a specific area and make foolish decisions. Faith means wholeheartedly trusting God with your current situation while you consistently sow & make wise financial decisions.

Be careful not to allow your faith to become your crutch. It is pretty easy to fall into a mindset where you are trusting and believing in God but doing nothing to activate your faith in

His Word. When we pray for something, it will almost never come in the form that we think it should come. T.D. Jakes once said, "God didn't make chairs, but He did give us trees." It is up to us to take it further. Put to work the God-given ideas and turn your dreams into reality. If we do not know how to move forward, we should pray and ask God for wisdom and resources. YouTube and Google are full of resources. Literally you can google, "How do I…" for anything.

Faith allows God to connect us with the right people and opportunities that we need to be successful. However, being that we each have free-will, if we do not do our part, we will not receive them.

Alternatively, sometimes our human nature will cause us to feel down because of the way we are viewing another person's blessings. It is important to shift perspectives and remain faithful to the promises of God. God examines each of our hearts. If you are in your seed-time, the period where you are sowing and expecting manifestation from God, remain faithful! If you are in your harvest, rejoice and save for the future. Many times we are ashamed of our current situation or we feel that our finances are our "personal business". You should not be too proud or too ashamed to seek the help of a financial advisor. This is where wisdom comes in. Do your research!

It is important that we use the resources that are available to us so that we can secure our finances and prepare for the next generation.

Building Generational Wealth

Generational wealth is not just a term to be thrown around loosely. Building generational wealth looks like passing down assets to family members, having them keep things intact, and continuously benefiting from those assets over time. The foundation that you set affects your children. It starts with you. What are your current financial practices? How do you build credit and pay off debts? Some people take on the "snowball effect" in which they pay off their higher interest cards first while others make minimum payments on all debts then use their extra funds to pay off the debt with the highest interest rate. In the approach that you choose, be sure that you are consistent. Establish good habits now, even if you start small, and you will see them pay off later.

Have you ever heard the phrase, "If you give a man a fish and you can feed him for a day, but if you teach a man how to fish, you can feed him for a lifetime"? It is imperative that you educate your children on the hard work, diligence, and dedication that building, establishing, and maintaining generation wealth requires. Let's discuss the different ways that you can obtain generational wealth while ensuring that you are protected and taken care of for life.

Financial Planning

Letsmakeaplan.org is a website that connects individuals with financial advisors and planning professionals. According to their website, their CFP® professionals have attained the standard of excellence in financial planning by meeting education, experience, and ethical standards, and as part of their certification, they have made a commitment to CFP Board to serve your best interests today to prepare you for a more secure tomorrow. Whether you are seeking one-time advice or a more detailed road map for your financial future, a CFP® professional is your ally. CFPs® cover six areas, including retirement planning, tax planning, investing, debt management, insurance planning, and estate planning.

When you hire a CFP® professional, you are hiring a trusted advisor who has committed to the CFP Board to put your interests first. That's because as part of their certification, a CFP® professional commits to acting as a fiduciary—which means acting in your best interests at all times when providing you with financial advice and financial planning services. A CFP® professional can receive sanctions from CFP Board, and even risk losing their certification, for violating this standard.

The process of working with a CFP® has been listed:

The First Meeting

At your first meeting, you'll usually discuss the financial planning process, what you would like to accomplish and how your CFP® professional can help you. Your advisor knows that the first step is to discuss the services that he or she will provide you, give you information on his or her background, detail how you will pay for products and services, detail how they will be compensated, and disclose any conflicts of interest.

Financial Planning

Once you agree to the scope of the financial planning engagement, including any conflicts of interest, the next step is for your CFP® professional to begin providing financial planning. Their first job is to gather information about your current finances and talk with you about your needs, priorities, and goals. This is the time to discuss issues such as risk tolerance and your exposure to longevity, economic, liability, and healthcare risks.

Analyzing Current Financial Strengths and Weaknesses

Your CFP® professional will want to analyze the strengths and vulnerabilities of your current financial situation and course of action. Depending upon your personal circumstances, this includes your cash flow, asset protection, employee benefits, emergency fund, and other financial data.

Developing Financial Planning Recommendations

The next step is to develop recommendations to help you meet your goals, explain the assumptions that are used to develop the plan, and offer alternatives. When he or she presents that plan, the process is designed to give you the opportunity to provide feedback and ask questions.

Executing the Financial Plan

Now it is time to put the plan into action. If your planning agreement includes implementation and monitoring, you will need a timeline for implementation, as well as details defining what will be monitored and how often, and when the recommendations will be updated.

A Collaborative Effort

You will need to work together to review the performance and progress of the plan over time. When there are changes in your personal circumstances (such as a change in employment or family status), that may call for adjustments to your plan. Throughout the process, your CFP® professional is able to provide ongoing support, guidance, and education.

Your CFP® professional knows that the first step in a thorough review is to assess where you stand currently, and then work with you to develop your goals. From there, your CFP® professional can help you make a plan designed to reach your goals, guide you through it, and then review your progress over time. Not every relationship is the same, and your plan may evolve as your life changes, but this is the process that your CFP® professional has been trained to follow.

According to SmartAsset, fee-based advisors could be helpful for people who don't want to work with multiple financial professionals though. If you want to buy insurance from the same person who created your financial plan, some fee-based advisors can do that for you. You also simply might have an advisor you like who happens to be fee-based. Just make sure to ask if your advisor is bound by fiduciary duty when acting as an advisor, as this guarantees that they must put their clients' best interests before their own.

Understanding Stocks & Bonds

It is no secret that the lack of participation from the African American community in stocks and investing is scarce until very recently. Research shows that less than forty percent of African Americans participate in stock investing. Do you believe that the absence of the mass majority of African Americans was simply due to the lack of resources and education held in our communities? The New York Times reported that Black families hold only five dollars and four cents for every one hundred dollars in white family's wealth; not even ten percent. While it is hardly ever discussed, African

American households earning over two hundred thousand dollars annually are among one of the fastest-growing groups in the United States. With the majority of the African American population not currently falling under that same category, and the mass media failing to highlight the financial progression in the African American community, it is important to know that it is achievable. Financial wellness does not begin and end with stocks. Each individual should try to include a variety of wealth-building investment strategies to their portfolios to increase diversification. Building wealth involves more than working and saving money.

Interest Rates

According to Investopedia, a low-interest rate environment occurs when the risk-free rate of interest, typically set by a central bank, is lower than the historic average for a prolonged period of time. In the United States, the risk-free rate is generally defined by the interest rate on Treasury securities. Seeing phrases like "zero interest rates" and "negative interest rates" are two extreme examples of low-interest rate environments. The Federal Reserve lowers interest rates in order to stimulate growth during a period of economic decline. That means that borrowing costs become cheaper. This is great for homeowners because it reduces their monthly mortgage payments. Similarly, prospective homeowners might be enticed into the market because of the cheaper costs. Low-interest rate environments benefit borrowers at the expense of the lenders and are meant to stimulate the economy by making it more accessible for individuals to borrow money from financial institutions.

Insurance

Are you currently insured? If you are not, have you ever considered your options in case of emergencies? As time passes and we increase in age, it is important to include insurance in our financial plans. We grow older, build businesses, get married, and start families. If anything were to ever happen to us or our loved ones, it would be sickening to think that we could not assist them more closely with the help of insurance.

Having insurance is a great way to pay off outstanding debts like credit cards and car loans. Additionally, having insurance is especially useful in the event of a death or an emergency. There are many types of insurance products. A few to consider are life insurance plans, home insurance, health insurance, and term insurance, but there are tons more. The three main types of insurance coverage include health, liability, and life insurance. Health insurance ensures that you, and your family, can receive adequate healthcare treatment and prescriptions at little to no cost to the individual. When enrolled in a health insurance policy, the majority of medical costs are paid for by the insurance company. As the insured, you will pay a premium regularly which will serve as your payment toward any medical or health-threatening emergencies that may arise. Health insurance can cover overnight hospitalization, daycare expenses, postoperative visits, and so much more. Liability insurance covers damages related to property, businesses, cars, homes, and other physical objects. If a property has been damaged, the insurance company pays the policyholder for whatever has occurred. Life insurance plans are necessary in protecting your family and financial interests during times of unfortunate and unexpected need.

The concept of insurance may seem like a complex matter, but it is extremely simple to understand. Upon enrolling in an insurance plan, you will pay a monthly or yearly fee to ensure that you will be financially protected in the event of unexpected damages or accidents. If something were to happen, say you were to total your car in a car accident, depending on your insurance plan the insurer will pay the financial damages for the harmed individual or property. Many people may look at purchasing insurance as an unnecessary expense or bill but consider this… What if one sudden emergency had the potential to wipe out over a year's worth of savings? Would it be worth it to get insurance just so that you can save your money in the long run? Absolutely! When seeking out insurance, it is important to determine your policy based upon the benefits you will receive as a policyholder, the requirements for remaining insured, and the affordability of the premium in relation to your other expenses.

According to the American Heart Association, 720,000 Americans suffer a heart attack annually, and somebody has a stroke every 40 seconds. The American Cancer Society states that there is a 33 percent chance for both men and women of developing cancer in their lifetimes. Just as troubling is the fact that 66% of all bankruptcies in the United States are tied to medical bills. Critical illness insurance helps you to cover outstanding expenses associated with serious, or critical, illnesses. Many individuals believe that they are fully covered for all emergencies with a standard health insurance plan but many of the costs associated with life-threatening illnesses and incidents carry a much higher bill than the normal accident. When you or your loved one is involved in a serious accident, critical illness coverage provides you with a lump-sum benefit of $10,000 to $50,000 in benefits initially upon receiving the diagnosis. Critical illness insurance policies cover heart attacks, cancer, strokes, kidney failures, heart transplants, paralysis, and related conditions.

There are three basic forms of critical illness: simplified issue, fully underwritten, and policy rider. A simplified issue critical illness insurance policy for individuals is affordable to most families and available in amounts up to $50,000. The underwriting requirements are not as strenuous as they would be for a critical care policy and only basic health questions are asked to obtain this type of insurance. Simplified issue critical illness insurance can also be purchased by independent insurance agents. Fully underwritten individual insurance is available for purchase through employers. You can purchase a fully underwritten critical illness insurance policy starting at amounts of up to $500,000. Due to the higher amount of protection, a more detailed account of your medical history is required. Policy rider insurance is available in the instance that critical illness coverage has been made available through an endorsement to the policy, also known as "policy rider". Upon purchasing a critical illness policy, the maximum lifetime benefit is chosen. When necessary, the policyholder is diagnosed with a condition that is covered under the policy. Then, critical insurance pays the benefit to the policyholder while they recover from the illness. Finances from the policyholder can be used to cover mortgage and rent costs, groceries, out-of-pocket medical costs, prescriptions, transportation to and from medical facilities, specialist treatments, and so much more. The American Association for Critical Illness Insurance recommends each individual to have enough coverage to make their mortgage payments for up to 4 weeks. The amount of money that you pay for critical illness insurance coverage depends on the risk that you pose to the insurance provider. It is safe to assume that the younger and healthier you are, the lower your premium coverage will be. However, it is important to note a few things. Women generally receive lower rates than men, costs of insurance vary based upon geographical location, if you use nicotine your rates will increase.

Real Estate Investment

Investing in real estate is one of the most popular ways to diversify an investment portfolio. Real estate is such a lucrative investment because the value of land will always increase over time. Real estate investors earn income through rental properties, appreciation, and profits secured through business activities that depend on the property. Real estate investment ensures passive income, portfolio diversification, a stable cash flow, and so much more. Additionally, REITs offer a few ways that you can invest in real estate without you having to own, operate, or finance any properties.

Here are a few reasons why you should get started in real estate investment today:

Fairly Easy to Get Started

Unlike most opportunities for wealth, you do not need a background in real estate or finance to begin investing.

High Tangible Asset Value

Land never loses its value, unlike stocks and bonds. According to the National Association of Realtors, real estate appreciation levels have held steady at 6 percent per year since 1968. The demand for land is constantly on an upward journey. With the population increasing year after year, land is becoming more of a limited resource. Securing real estate investments and holding on to them can ensure much financial success, even during times of economic hardship. Moreover, investors who hang onto their real estate investments during recessions have seen the value of their properties return back to normal within a few years.

Plenty of Financing Options

There are numerous ways to finance a real estate purchase. You can use cash, traditional mortgage loans, angel investors, or residential hard money loans. With this type of flexibility, you have the power to choose the method that fits your current financial situation the best.

Tax Benefits

As an investor in real estate, you technically are running a business. As a business owner, you are entitled to a plethora of tax exemptions and benefits. Take a look at the tax advantages associated with rental income, mortgage interest, management expenses, operating costs, insurance expenses, property taxes, and depreciation.

Steady Income

If you decide to secure a real estate investment for rentals, then you have the potential to receive passive income every month. Imagine landing a high-quality property with tenants who can afford to pay more. Your passive income would definitely increase monthly and the good news is, you can spend your money however you would like to! Another thing to point out is the leverage offered by your real estate investments. For example, you can use $200,000 in leverage assets to purchase three properties with down payments, instead of purchasing one for $100,000 in cash. Be sure to do your research so that you can learn and understand the ways that leverage can impact your future real estate deals.

Competitive Risk-Adjusted Returns

Risk-adjusted return measures how much risk is involved in producing a particular return. Being that real estate investments are less volatile than traditional investments like stocks and bonds, so they are not as likely to shift unpredictably. The real estate market remains consistent so investors can take advantage of their stable costs and relatively smooth returns.

While these were only a few, there are so many more great reasons to invest in real estate. Take a look at some real estate investment strategies and start setting yourself up for financial freedom!

Here are a few helpful resources to assist you on your home ownership journey:

NACA Homeownership Program
https//www.naca.com
425-602-6222

HUD
https//www.hud.gov/hudprograms
202-708-1112

Habitat for Humanity
https//habitat.org
1-800-habitat
229-924-6935

For individuals living with disabilities:

Dreamscape Foundation
www.dreamscapefoundation.com
239-325-1881

Rebuilding Together, Americorps

www.rebuildingtogether.org

1-800-473-4229

Low to moderate-income housing:

United Family Network

www.unitedfamilynetwork.com

703-684-7722

800-969-6642

Volunteers of America

www.voa.org

703-341-5000

Real Estate Investment Trusts

The National Association of Real Estate Investment Trust (NAREIT) defines a real estate investment trust (REIT) as a company that owns, operates, or finances income-producing real estate. REITs provide all investors the chance to own valuable real estate, present the opportunity to access dividend-based income and total returns, and help communities grow, thrive, and revitalize.

REITs allow anyone to invest in portfolios of real estate assets the same way they invest in other industries – through the purchase of individual company stock or a mutual fund or exchange-traded fund (ETF). The stockholders of a REIT earn a share of the income produced through real estate investment – without actually having to go out and buy, manage or finance a property. Approximately 145 million Americans invest in REIT stocks through their 401(k) and other investment funds.

In total, REITs of all types collectively own more than $3.5 trillion in gross assets across the U.S., with stock-exchange listed REITs owning approximately $2.5 trillion in assets, representing more than 500,000 properties. The United States listed REITs have an equity market capitalization of more than $1 trillion.

REITs invest in a wide scope of real estate property types, including offices, apartment buildings, warehouses, retail centers, medical facilities, data centers, cell towers, infrastructure, and hotels. Most REITs focus on a particular property type, but some hold multiple types of properties in their portfolios.

Listed REIT assets are categorized into one of 13 property sectors:

Office

Industrial

Retail

Lodging/Resorts

Residential

Timberlands

Health Care

Self-storage

Infrastructure

Data Centers

Diversified

Specialty

Mortgage

Most REITs operate under a straightforward and easily understandable business model: By leasing space and collecting rent on its real estate, the company generates income which is then paid out to shareholders in the form of dividends. REITs must payout at least 90 % of their taxable income to shareholders—and must pay out 100 %. In turn, shareholders pay income taxes on those dividends.

Mortgage REITs (or mREITs) don't own real estate directly, instead, they finance real estate and earn income from the interest on these investments.

Historically, REITs have delivered competitive total returns that were based on high, steady dividend income and long-term capital appreciation. The existing, and dramatically, low correlation with other assets also makes them an excellent addition to any portfolio because it helps a person to reduce overall portfolio risk and increase returns.

There are three types of Real Estate Investment Trusts:

Equity REITs: own or operate income-producing real estate. Often referred to by professionals, simply, like REITs. The majority of REITs are publicly traded equity REITs.

mREITs: also known as mortgage REITs, provide financing for income-producing real estate by purchasing or originating mortgages and mortgage-backed securities and earning income from the interest on these investments.

Public Non-listed REITs: registered with the Securities and Exchange Commission but do not trade on national stock exchanges.

Private REITs: offerings that are exempt from the Securities and Exchange Commission registration and whose shares do not trade on national stock exchanges.

The National Association of Investors Corporation (NAIC) is a nonprofit organization dedicated to providing investor education and promoting investor success. The NAIC was founded in 1951. The association is based in Madison Heights, Michigan, and is composed of investing clubs along with individual investors from all around the United States. Today, the organization goes by the name BetterInvesting.

The National Association of Investors Corporation stresses four principles for successful, long-term investing:

Invest regularly, regardless of market conditions

Reinvest all earnings

Invest in growth companies (and growth mutual funds)

Diversify to reduce risk

The National Association of Investors Corporation has a member's magazine subscription called BetterInvesting, the common, branded name for the association since 2004. The organization's mission is to educate individuals on the benefits of long-term investing in common stocks. With the popularity of 401(k)s and other defined-contribution retirement plans already in existence, education regarding stock and bond mutual funds became the newest additions.

Members of the NAIC have access to online tools for determining whether a stock is that of a quality growth company and is selling at a price that will provide sufficient potential return. Additionally, members receive access to educational webinars, First Cut stock studies contributed by the BetterInvesting community, print copies of BetterInvesting Magazine, local chapter support, and access to a wide range of products and services.

Diversifying A Portfolio

According to Fidelity, diversification is the practice of spreading your investments around so that your exposure to any one type of asset is limited. This practice is designed to help reduce the volatility of your portfolio over time. A lower volatility means that the value of one's security, or investments, will continue steadily rather than constantly changing dramatically. According to Investopedia, diversification is a battle cry for many financial planners, fund managers, and individual investors alike. It is a management strategy that blends different investments in a single portfolio. The idea behind diversification is that a variety of investments will yield a higher return. It also suggests that investors will face lower risk by investing in different vehicles.

Listed below are five tips for helping you to diversify your portfolio:

Spread the Wealth

Equities can be wonderful, but don't put all of your money in one stock or one sector. Consider creating your own virtual mutual fund by investing in a handful of companies you know, trust and even use in your day-to-day life.

But stocks aren't just the only thing to consider. You can also invest in commodities, exchange-traded funds (ETFs), and real estate investment trusts (REITs). And don't just stick to your home base. Think beyond it and go global. This way, you'll spread your risk around, which can lead to bigger rewards.

People will argue that investing in what you know will leave the average investor too heavily retail-oriented, but knowing a company, or using its goods and services, can be a healthy and wholesome approach to this sector.

Still, don't fall into the trap of going too far. Make sure you keep yourself to a portfolio that's manageable. There's no sense in investing in 100 different vehicles when you don't have the time or resources to keep up. Try to limit yourself to about 20 to 30 different investments.

Consider Index or Bond Funds

You may want to consider adding index funds or fixed-income funds to the mix. Investing in securities that track various indexes makes a wonderful long-term diversification investment for your portfolio. By adding some fixed-income solutions, you are further hedging your portfolio against market volatility and uncertainty. These funds try to match the performance of broad indexes, so rather than investing in a specific sector, they try to reflect the bond market's value.

These funds often come with low fees, which is another bonus. It means more money in your pocket. The management and operating costs are minimal because of what it takes to run these funds.

Keep Building Your Portfolio

Add to your investments on a regular basis. If you have $10,000 to invest, use dollar-cost averaging. This approach is used to help smooth out the peaks and valleys created by market volatility. The idea behind this strategy is to cut down your investment risk by investing the same amount of money over a period of time.

With dollar-cost averaging, you invest money regularly into a specified portfolio of securities. Using this strategy, you'll buy more shares when prices are low, and fewer when prices are high.

Know When to Get Out

Buying and holding and dollar-cost averaging are sound strategies. But just because you have your investments on autopilot doesn't mean you should ignore the forces at work.

Stay current with your investments and stay abreast of any changes in overall market conditions. You'll want to know what is happening to the companies you invest in. By doing so, you'll also be able to tell when it's time to cut your losses, sell and move on to your next investment.

Keep a Watchful Eye on Commissions

If you are not the trading type, understand what you are getting for the fees you are paying. Some firms charge a monthly fee, while others charge transaction fees. These can definitely add up and chip away at your bottom line.

Be aware of what you are paying and what you are getting for it. Remember, the cheapest choice is not always the best. Keep yourself updated on whether there are any changes to your fees.

According to Fidelity, one of the keys to successful investing is learning how to balance your comfort level with risk against your time horizon. Invest your retirement nest egg too conservatively at a young age, and you run the risk that the growth rate of your investments won't keep pace with inflation. Conversely, if you invest too aggressively when you're older, you could leave your savings exposed to market volatility, which could erode the value of your assets at an age when you have fewer opportunities to recoup your losses.

Here are the four primary components of a diversified portfolio:

Domestic stocks: stocks represent the most aggressive portion of your portfolio and provide the opportunity for higher growth over the long term. However, this greater potential for growth carries a greater risk, particularly in the short term. Because stocks are generally more volatile than other types of assets, your investment in a stock could be worthless if and when you decide to sell it.

Bonds: most bonds provide regular interest income and are generally considered to be less volatile than stocks. They can also act as a cushion against the unpredictable ups and downs of the stock market, as they often behave differently than stocks. Investors who are more focused on safety, rather than growth, often favor the United States Treasury or other high-quality bonds, while reducing their exposure to stocks. These investors may have to accept lower long-term returns, as many bonds—especially high-quality issues—generally don't offer returns as high as stocks over the long term. However, note that some fixed-income investments, like high-yield bonds and certain international bonds, can offer much higher yields, albeit with more risk.

Short-term investments: these include money market funds and short-term CDs (certificates of deposit). Money market funds are conservative investments that offer stability and easy access to your money, ideal for those looking to preserve principal. In exchange for that level of safety, money market funds usually provide lower returns than bond funds or individual bonds. While money market funds are considered safer and more conservative, however, they are not insured or guaranteed by the Federal Deposit Insurance Corporation (FDIC) the way many CDs are. When you invest in CDs though, you may sacrifice the liquidity generally offered by money market funds.

You could lose money by investing in a money market fund or any investment for that matter. Although the fund seeks to preserve the value of your investment at $1.00 per share, it cannot guarantee it will do so. The Fund may impose a fee upon the sale of your shares or may temporarily suspend your ability to sell shares if the Fund's liquidity falls below required minimums because of market conditions or other factors. An investment in the fund is not insured or guaranteed by the Federal Deposit Insurance Corporation or any other government agency. Fidelity Investments and its affiliates, the fund's sponsor, have no legal obligation to provide financial support to the fund, and you should not expect that the sponsor will provide financial support to the fund at any time.

International stocks: stocks issued by non-US companies often perform differently than their US counterparts, providing exposure to opportunities not offered by US securities. If you're searching for investments that offer both higher potential returns and higher risk, you may want to consider adding some foreign stocks to your portfolio.

Additional components of a diversified portfolio include:

Sector funds: although these invest in stocks, sector funds, as their name suggests, focus on a particular segment of the economy. They can be valuable tools for investors seeking opportunities in different phases of the economic cycle.

Commodity-focused funds: while only the most experienced investors should invest in commodities, adding equity funds that focus on commodity-intensive industries to your portfolio—such as oil and gas, mining, and natural resources—can provide a good hedge against inflation.

Real estate funds: real estate funds, including real estate investment trusts (REITs), can also play a role in diversifying your portfolio and providing some protection against the risk of inflation.

Asset allocation funds: for investors who don't have the time or the expertise to build a diversified portfolio, asset allocation funds can serve as an effective single-fund strategy. Fidelity manages a number of different types of these funds, including funds that are managed to a specific target date, funds that are managed to maintain a specific asset allocation, funds that are managed to generate income, and funds that are managed in anticipation of specific outcomes, such as inflation.

Another common term that you may hear when discussing diversifying a portfolio is "rebalancing". According to the Securities and Exchange Commission, rebalancing is bringing your portfolio back to your original asset allocation mix. This is necessary because over time some of your investments may become out of alignment with your investment goals. You'll find that some of your investments will grow faster than others. By rebalancing, you'll ensure that your portfolio does not overemphasize one or more asset categories, and you'll return your portfolio to a comfortable level of risk.

For example, let's say you determined that stock investments should represent 60% of your portfolio. But after a recent stock market increase, stock investments represent 80% of your portfolio. You'll need to either sell some of your stock investments or purchase investments from an under-weighted asset category to reestablish your original asset allocation mix.

When you rebalance, you'll also need to review the investments within each asset allocation category. If any of these investments are out of alignment with your investment goals, you'll need to make changes to bring them back to their original allocation within the asset category.

There are basically three different ways you can rebalance your portfolio:

You can sell off investments from over-weighted asset categories and use the proceeds to purchase investments for under-weighted asset categories.

You can purchase new investments for under-weighted asset categories.

If you are making continuous contributions to the portfolio, you can alter your contributions so that more investments go to under-weighted asset categories until your portfolio is back into balance.

Before you rebalance your portfolio, you should consider whether the method of rebalancing you decide to use will trigger transaction fees or tax consequences. Your financial professional or tax adviser can help you identify ways that you can minimize these potential costs.

You can choose to rebalance your portfolio depending on your investments or your personal time clock. Financial experts recommend that investors get into the habit of rebalancing their portfolios regularly, on an interval. A great example of this would be to rebalance your portfolio every six or twelve months. Other researchers advise rebalancing only when the relative weight of an asset class grows or decreases more than a certain percentage that you've identified in advance.

The bottom line is, investing can be educational, entertaining, and enjoyable. By deciding to take a disciplined approach with your investments, you will be able to continue on the upward side of investing even during the worst times. While diversification does not ensure a profit or guarantee a loss, it can mitigate the risk and volatility of your portfolio. By doing so, you can reduce the number of ups and downs in the investment life cycle.

401(k) Explained

When it comes to retirement plans, research has found that the typical White family holds over one hundred thousand dollars in liquid savings for retirement while the average African American only holds around nineteen thousand dollars in retirement savings. An article written by Forbes revealed that the average balance of African American savings into a 401(k) plan is only around twenty thousand dollars. While age and salary are two of the main factors in retirement savings, ethnicity and lack of education play a huge role in the participation of African Americans in retirement plans. Statistically speaking, African Americans are less likely to participate in their employer's 401(k) plans; when they do participate, they typically save at lower rates than Whites. Alternatively, Asian American employees were said to have the highest 401(k) participation and savings rates among all racial groups. With lower participation rates, combined with higher withdrawal rates, smaller account balances have been found among African American employees. As an employee, it is very important for you to do your research on your retirement savings plan to ensure that you are taking full advantage of the resources made available to you by your employer. 401(k) plans are voluntary, meaning that it is the employee's choice to enroll in the program. Being that African Americans have a significantly lower amount of wealth than other racial groups, it is very difficult to opt into a program that takes money away from each paycheck for long-term goals, especially if income is already low. 83% of African Americans do not have the proper finances to set aside for retirement savings, and 75% of African Americans have less than ten thousand dollars in their retirement savings accounts. To improve these statistics, consider educating yourself and speaking with a financial advisor to discuss your options, regardless of your income level. Take advantage of your employer's 401(k) plan fully, especially if the employer has a matching contribution program in place. When you contribute at the amount that the employer is matching, you have the potential to double the savings that you have toward retirement. Your taxable income is also lowered, due to the lessened amount of income received from each paycheck. In addition to enrolling in your employer's 401(k) plan, consider opening a Roth IRA account as well. Combining your Roth IRA with your 401(k) contributions ensures that you receive immediate tax savings, along with the option to make tax-free withdrawals from your Roth IRA account. In 2014, statistics discovered that African American private-sector employees earned only 78% of the income awarded to their fellow white employees. In the public sector, African American employees earned 90% of the wages given to their white counterparts. Public pension income is important to African Americans intending to retire, more so than any other racial group. In the same year, research revealed that Social Security Income and public pensions accounted for 57% of African American income for retirees, compared to 49% for White retirees. Social Security Income and public pension income has accounted for 63% of total retirement savings for African American women, being the highest share of any race and gender in the United States. By comparison, 51% of African American men received 51% of their savings from these retirement sources. Employees of color are less likely to have an employer-sponsored retirement plan or individual retirement account, in comparison to other racial groups. 54% of African American employees work for employers that sponsor retirement plans, versus 62% of White employees and 38% of Hispanic employees. This concern exists much more prevalently in the private sector of employment. African Americans do not have access to the same coverage by pensions that ensure lifetime retirement income. While 24% of White employees currently have a pension program in place through their current employers, only 16% of African American employees do. Only 15% of African Americans have access to a private-sector job providing retirement plans, compared to 42% of White households. 62% of African American households do not have assets in a retirement account and African American employees do not place the same importance, or dedication, to the building of a retirement savings account. Sadly, African American households only hold 25% of the retirement income that White households have. It is important to educate yourself on your retirement savings options and carve out the time, and finances, to begin building on your future. Ensure that you are not frivolously spending or making unnecessary purchases. Save money, even in small amounts, and remember that the money will add up. In the case of a financial emergency, always prepare a plan to avoid debt. Having a secure plan for the future in place is way better than being unprepared.

Wills and Trusts

If you have assets and, or children, it is imperative that you do a little estate planning. Avoiding estate planning can leave a family susceptible to being in debt after a loved one passes if they were not properly prepared. Unfortunately, in some communities this topic is not discussed enough, instead we rely on the older or trusted sibling to handle these responsibilities. You should think about trusts and wills as vehicles to ensure that your family is taken care of after death. According to the Hanscom Federal Credit Union, a will is a legal document that instructs how you want your assets (financial and material) distributed after your death. In it you can appoint your executor/executrix/personal representative, name your beneficiaries, designate guardians for your children, and leave specific instructions as to how and when your beneficiaries receive their inheritances. What people don't always understand is that wills are submitted to the probate court governing where the decedent last lived (a trust lets you avoid this, but we'll get to that in a minute). While the idea of probate court might sound scary, it really isn't. All the probate court judge will do is ensure the will is legal and valid. A valid will also gives the person you designate as your executor the legal right to administer your estate, allowing them to move forward with tasks like resolving outstanding financial liabilities and distributing assets to your beneficiaries.

A trust is a legal entity, existing for the sole purpose of protecting the assets in your estate. Typically, trusts are recommended for people with significant assets, in part because they can be expensive to create and administer, often upwards of $5,000. You might still need a will for things like appointing a guardian for your children, but a trust will cover your estate's finances and allow the details of your finances to remain private, as a trust passes outside of probate.

While a will determines how your assets will be distributed after you die, a trust becomes the legal owner of your assets the moment the trust is created. There are numerous types of trusts out there, but an irrevocable trust is most relevant in the world of personal estate planning. As the name implies, an irrevocable trust cannot be revoked once it is created; in other words, if you put a property in the trust, you cannot take it out. This is ideal for people who want to avoid probate and keep the details of their estates private. Wills are public record. An irrevocable trust also allows you to make more detailed provisions regarding the use of your estate, as well as offers you protection from creditors or potential litigants. In the book "Rich Dad, Poor Dad", Robert Kiyosaki states, "You're only poor if you give up. The most important thing is that you did something. Most people only talk and dream of getting rich. You've done something." As long as you take the first steps toward building the generational wealth that you envision, you have begun a great journey toward the land of financial freedom.

Afterthought

Apostle Tommy Brown did a teaching called "Access Denied" and our obedience to God determines the level of access we give Him in our lives. When God has access to your life, He will give you wisdom beyond our natural limits, allowing us to see beyond what we can see.

Dr. Tony Evans said, "If all you see is what you see, then you have not seen all there is to see." Obedience to God allows His hand to move in our lives, He will give us wisdom in what to do and how to do it. On the contrary, disobedience can place you in a situation where you can lose out on opportunities for financial increase. Disobedience can also cause you to fall into a financial ditch. Giving God access extends beyond the church pew, it applies to every single area of your life.

How does this relate to our finances? Wealth = influence! Imagine how we can impact policies, procedures, media, and education if we had a voice!

Let's take it one step further. Peter's problem was paying his taxes, through his obedience he was able to not only pay his taxes but to pay someone else's taxes. Reflect on that. You can be a financial blessing to someone else through your obedience.

Joseph's wisdom, through his relationship (obedience) to God, put him in a position to solve problems. Pharaoh had a problem and Joseph was the solution. Why? Because he had given God access to his life; God gave Joseph a solution and as Pharoah heeded the instruction, was able to preserve his nation and provide resources to other nations.

Both men were obedient, followed instructions, and in turn, were able to be a blessing to another. When your why becomes bigger than you, your intentions and motives for finances will change and will be for the greater good. The financial increase will come to you for resources for the nations and not just for selfish pleasures.

www.ingramcontent.com/pod-product-compliance
Lightning Source LLC
Chambersburg PA
CBHW070429180526
45158CB00017B/943